TRILOGY

Also by H.D.

TRILOGY

The Walls Do Not Fall
Tribute to the Angels
The Flowering of the Rod

by H.D.

CARCANET

First published in 1973, third impression in 1997 by
Carcanet Press Limited
4th Floor, Conavon Court
12–16 Blackfriars Street
Manchester M3 5BQ

A CIP catalogue record for this book
is available from the British Library.
ISBN 1 85754 316 5

The publisher acknowledges financial assistance from the
Arts Council of England.

Printed and bound in England by SRP Ltd, Exeter

FOREWORD

The publisher's statement on the page-proofs of *The Walls Do
Not Fall* (1944) began, "H.D. was at one time well known to all
lovers of verse as one of the earliest 'Imagists'." Firmly, H.D.
crossed out "was at one time". Over it she wrote "IS". She, any-
how, remembered. She, now, preferred the present tense. She had
been silent as a poet but the air raids of World War Two, the
"incidents" as the press ironically called the bombings, and the
disappearance from London squares of railings to be melted into
munitions, brought first desolation and then inspiration. "The orgy
of destructions . . . to be witnessed and lived through in London,"
she wrote, as I quoted in my foreword to *Hermetic Definition* (1972),
"that outer threat and constant reminder of death drove me in-
ward". So did war for Eliot in his *Four Quartets*, and did for Edith
Sitwell in poems like "Still Falls the Rain". They had found some-
thing to say. They were energized. This was a civilians' war for
English-speaking people in a sense that war had never been before,
not for civilian poets certainly. The experience was new. The
poems were fresh. The chiefly memorable poetry from this war is
by civilians; Pound's *Pisan Cantos* can be included. But the poems
are of course about much more than war.

The experience of the raids was apocalyptic, a recurrence of
the testimony of Saint John in *The Book of Revelation*. "One seems,"
H.D. wrote me in August of 1943, "to shed a skin or husk, once in
so often—a biological process—in fact, the whole race has got to
slough off, out of it—the past I mean—and this 'new creation' is
already on us."

I was in London. I stood guard on the roofs. I saw the night sky
made fiercely bright by magnesium flares, heard the drone of enemy
raiders, felt the flack, and saw the city circled by flame. I saw the
bombs' knife-edge slice through houses to dissect them. These were
not dolls-houses nor museum exhibits (though like them). They
were today's history. One was living in the agony of spirit.

The Walls Do Not Fall was dedicated to her friend Bryher, "for
Karnak" where they had been together, "from London" where
they were experiencing the war. They had seen the temple of
Amen-Ra, had been in Egypt at the moment of the excavation of
Tutankhamen whom, in the statue now in the Louvre, Amen holds

between his legs. Those temples and shrines lay open to the sky; so now did fragments of London. H.D. was trying to connect the experience of World War Two with her history and with history in general. This was spiritual etymology. Behind Egypt and Amen was Mithra. Ahead of Egypt was Christianity; Amen became, in the Bible, Christ. Ahead of the Goat's horns was the Age of Aquarius (the Waterman). "I wish Aquarius would get born before we perish," she wrote a friend. The bennu bird, the Egyptian phoenix, dropped a grain in the small urn of the heart. The grain grew to a rod. The rod promised a blossom. We are still, H.D. affirmed, the "latter-day twice-born". "Resurrection could occur in life, as in death," she wrote elsewhere. This is not simply the sense of John's baptism of Christ, but an aspect of what H.D. calls "spiritual realism". It is the example of the cocoon, spun from *Psalm* 22, "But I am a worm, and no man". Karnak and London, linked, explain "symbols of the past in today's imagery".

Writing to me about the poems in the first group of what she later referred to simply as *Trilogy*, she clarified them for me on a Sunday in 1943. "I do not want to pick out gems or be a 'clear-cut crystal'. That catch-phrase is easy for journalists. A seed is not a crystal—and if my mustard-seed has grown too high and spread too many branches, that is a pity for the critic, that is a pity for H.D. fans (few and far between though they are—but you wrote me, for instance, of some boy in the west). But that is it; for the boy in the west, you said, we must give candy and sweets, rather than bread—wine rather than water. Yes. Yes. I agree there. But for us, starved, suffocated—flung from our raft on the beleaguered rock—'this England'—or the rock of the latter-day falsity and *laisser-aller*, the between-wars, I mean—for us, water and 'baked fish'—you will find the 'baked fish' in XXIX. That is how it is—and too, in the very midst of the 'fifty thousand incidents' of the actual Blitz, there is that last desperate re-valuation or final valuation, I mean, here 'long ago', two years ago, we do not know if we live to tell the tale, but we still cling to our standards—to this, I mean, our PROFESSION. Now here it is, very stark and written at the last—a sort of vindication of the writer, or the 'scribe'—as in VIII for instance, that was really 'tapped out' in a sort of exhilaration of rage at the stupidity of someone who had written me from USA—and I do not blame them at all—someone who did not know and could not, what we were doing, how we had moreover been waiting for this to happen

vi

for years and years before it happened—some nice and kind and perceptive person, who remarked of a not-very-good-poet and of some not-very-good-poems, that after all, it did seem strange to think of anyone troubling to try to express world-issues now, it was really so 'pathetic'. It was the word 'pathetic', the sort of patting-on-the-head, the suave patronizing manner—that got me. Pathetic? O, yes, and now here, the serpent rears its head and it's a nice fanged little head with plenty of venom concealed—and it is hissing and coiling about, I think, stirred to hiss a few words, a 'few last words', maybe in defence of its 'brood'. Writers? Pathetic? 'Yes, of course,' it hisses but do you know that the writer is the original rune-maker, the majic-maker, his words are sacred—that is what it is. You speak of a second-rate writer—but you just be careful— the second-rate may become first-rate—and anyhow—well, it is there in VIII, hissing its way to the end and its terse statement that the scribe 'stands second only to the Pharaoh', or what it really means 'stands second only to God'—the Pharaoh actually being imbued with god-attributes.

"But it was an English girl who made me still madder—with a letter to Bryher at *Life and Letters* questioning the status of the poet, the writer in the future world-reconstruction—that is the 'non-utilitarian' touch in the same VIII . . . The parallel between ancient Egypt and 'ancient' London is obvious. In I the 'fallen roof leaves the sealed room open to the air' is of course true of our own house of life—outer violence touching the deepest hidden sub-conscious terrors, etc. and we see so much of our past 'on show', as it were 'another sliced wall where poor utensils show like rare objects in a museum'. Egypt? London? Mystery, majic—that I have found in London! The mystery of death, first and last— stressed in XL, XLI, XLII, Osiris being the spirit of the under-world, the sun under the world, the setting-sun, the end—implicit there always the idea of the sun-rise—and above all the ever-lasting miracle of the breath of life—

> where heat breaks and cracks
> the sand-waste
> you are a mist
> of snow: white, little flowers.

Then the end, XLIII.

"Osbert [Sitwell] seemed to like the way they were written, he wrote Bryher to the effect that H.D. had neatly set traps, that snapped shut with the inevitable and unexpected idea or *mot* at the end. (These are not his exact words.) But I liked O. liking them and I think he really did—he it was, who wrote Sir Humphrey Milford, I told you.

"I think IX is very neat, on re-reading.

"XXX, XXXI, XXXII may seem rather long—but oddly, XXXI, XXXII actually did tap-off all in one—rather startled me to write all that in one fell swoop and made no changes, save for ordinary tidying-up—it rather startled me, so I let the thing stand—it is a bit larger 'trap', I suppose, for a larger, bulkier animal—but it does snap-shut neatly—with (XXXII) 'you find all this?'

"Well, Norman, this long letter is too bad—I suppose this book is 'philosophy'. Now I start, I could go on, but please realise that I appreciate your interest. 'Protection for the scribe' seems to be the leit-motif. And the feeling of assurance back of it of the presence of the God of the Scribe,—Thoth, Hermes, Ancient-of-Days, Ancient Wisdom, *AMEN*. And exactly the place of the scribe in the mysteries of all-time—his 'job' as 'householder', XXXVI, his exact place in the sequence, in the pattern, again his 'job', the keeping-track of the 'treasures' which contain *for every scribe which is instructed, things new and old.*"

Readers also need to be instructed. Jesus was speaking to them too in *Matthew*. "I was working on the idea of the mysteries and the ruins of Egypt and the ruins of London," H.D. wrote of *The Walls Do Not Fall* in an unpublished novel, *Majic Ring*. Once the reader senses this he is off to a better start than those reviewers who thought she was now being true to the Egyptians as she had been said to be true to the Greeks. A better guide is Arthur Weigall's *The Paganism in Our Christianity* (1928), which was a favorite of hers and appropriately marked. But *The Book of Revelation* as well as the *Old Testament* and the *Gospels*, especially of John, are essential. Her italicized quotations are usually from them. The recurrence of jars and jasper and amber and Amen are reincarnations within the poem. We recognize the Magi not as Kings of the Orient but as the intellectually élite in the worship of Zoroaster and Mithra, possessing as Gilbert Vezin puts it in his *L'Adoration et Le Cycle des Mages* (1950), the sum of knowledge of their age: astrology, astronomy, medicine, mathematics and occult science. The Magi were Wise Men; they were Scribes. Kaspar's offering of myrrh was like the offering of a poem. Words, like the Word itself, themselves can be re-incarnations.

Osbert Sitwell did more than recommend to Sir Humphrey Milford the publication of *The Walls Do Not Fall*. He wrote a review of it for the *Observer*. H.D. sent a copy of the review to a cousin in America, Francis Wolle. He too had come from Bethlehem. "I like the review so much," she wrote in June 1944, "and the line, 'we want—we need—more' so be-dazzled me that I sat down the last two weeks of May and did another series, the same length [each of the Trilogy has 43 sections]; a sort of premature peace poem. I am so glad I got it done, as the news of the fall of Rome, followed up so soon after by the Day or the D-Day doings, has so completely upset us all—we feel completely subdued. . . ." The following April she repeated herself somewhat, when she was ready to send him *Tribute to the Angels* (1945): "I wrote it last spring in a wonderful pause just before D-Day. However, the worst came after, with the doodle-bugs or more politely buzz-bombs or fly-bombs. So perhaps the Angels did make a special effort to look after us—anyhow I owe them something. There is a Lady too—but she is the Troubadour's or Poet's Lady; anyhow, she put in an appearance—in a dream—in the middle of writing the sequence, so in she went to the book."

In December 1944 she had sent me, across London, a letter. The contracts had been signed. Sir Humphrey Milford said, "as soon as he could get the paper—I asked to have the format like *Walls*—he would have *Angels* set up". Her letter was mostly about the new poems: "I took a bus to Putney—the trees, etc. as per enclosed. I wrote the poems at odd moments, as a poet should—started the first, on the top of the bus brushing through those chestnut-trees. They link on to the first—I purposely tried to keep the link, but carry on from the black tunnel or darkness or 'initiation', at least towards the tunnel entrance. I really DID feel that a new heaven and a new earth were about to materialize. It lasted as you know, for a few weeks—then D-Day! And the 're-gathering, thundering storm'. The Angel names are more or less traditional O[ld] T[estament], though I use the Mohammedan name for the planet Saturn, ruler of time and death, Azrael. The Venus name, I believe is Anael but I spelt it ANNAEL; it didn't seem to 'work' until I did—it links on too with Anna, Hannah or Grace, so has an authentic old-testament angel ring. The italic-quotes are mostly from Revelation—one is from O.T. (XXIII [Gen. 48.16]). The one, XXVII, 'angels unawares' I think is Hebrews [13.2]. I think the others are all Revelations. The Latin in the last, *vas spirituale/ rosa mystica*—are from the Laurentian Litany to the Virgin, R.C. missal. I think [our friend] is wrong to say there is R.C. implication —I distinctly link the LADY up with Venus-Annael, with the Moon, with the pre-Christian Roman Bona Dea, with the Byzantine Greek church Santa Sophia and the SS of the Sanctus Spiritus. I say she is NOT even *vas spirituale/rosa mystica*—which is lovely poetry; *ora pro nobis*. Old Zadkiel is really our old Amen again—now having an angel-name; there is a traditional Zadkiel but do not know if mentioned in Writ—but there is Uriel, I believe, and some are named in the Apocryphal *Book of Enoch* which I can never place, though see quoted. I dedicated the book to O[sbert], as I told you, with the last lines of *Walls*."

In *Tribute to the Angels*, H.D. was moving forward and backward in spiritual realities. The twenty-first chapter of *The Book of Revelation* and its vision of a New Jerusalem blended with the green-white of the may-tree, the charred tree, "an ordinary tree in an old garden-square". "Never, never was a season more beautiful," more fully beautiful by contrast with devastation. From the green-white of the blossoms, as in a dreamed epiphany, comes "Our Lady universally", sensed over centuries in the differing dreams of artists. They are scribes with the brush. Now, to H.D., she had emerged once more.

Tribute to the Angels gives thanks for the services of the seven angels at the throne of God, un-named by Saint John and to-be-named by scribes later, like H.D. herself. Both her book and Saint John's are filled with cited sevens. Even the 43 sections of each third of H.D.'s *Trilogy* add up to seven. Half-concealed links are every-where. This is wit, this is a sense of one-ness. This is itself a tribute and not simply thanks.

There were only a few months between the *Tribute* and the final poems of the trilogy. In September 1944 she thanked me "for having read the Angel series. I want myself to 'do' something about it—either write a slight introduction or as you say leave it and do a third to the trilogy. . . . But as I haven't the foggiest of what the 3rd is to be about and am rather harassed and wrote the 2nd under compulsion—I don't know where I am. Have you any inspirational ideas?????"

But her ideas were seeds in the sections she had already written.

"The rod of power" was still to be recovered. "He is Mage, bringing myrrh" from *The Walls* was still to be fulfilled. In *Tribute* we are prepared for "a tale of a jar or jars". The apostrophe to Zadkiel, "This is the flowering of the rod," was to re-blossom in the presence of the infant Christ,—that is, in Life.

The Flowering of the Rod was beyond and above war. "We have done all that we could." Golgotha gives way to love and resurrection. All nature provides resemblance to divine things, reveals them as ancient wisdom does. The wild-geese in their instinctive flight affirm Paradise, as the Magi do in their unswerving response to the star. So also does Mary-of-Magdala when with her jar of ointment she washes His feet and is re-born. Her actions echo the lines from *The Walls*: "In me (the worm) clearly is no righteousness, but this—persistence." So Mary is persistent in obtaining Kaspar's other jar, he who as Mage had brought only one of his two to the manger. "Resurrection is a sense of direction."

H.D. wrote Mary-of-Magdala's story and that of Kaspar as though they were a part of the Kabala. As final lines to a rejected fifteenth section of the sequence, in a manuscript now in the Beinecke Library of Yale, she wrote of how the Rabbis "huddled over the Kabala" and scribbled later forbidden books. "Some say that the old proscribed Rabbis said that the Arab was God." As easily the Arab became Kaspar. How much of these two examples of unswerving response was H.D.'s artifice I do not know. Within the *Trilogy* they become verities.

Karnak and London were periods of H.D.'s history. So also were Bethlehem and Philadelphia, though they remain significant shadows in the *Trilogy*. Philadelphia was named by Penn certainly with *The Book of Revelation* in mind. The "spacious, bare meeting-house" of her dream of the "father of past aeons" in *The Walls*, she describes elsewhere as Quaker, "in or by Philadelphia", where her family worshipped when she was in her 'teens, there being no Moravian congregation conveniently near.

Bethlehem was her birthplace. In "Advent", an extension of her *Tribute to Freud*, she documents its significance to her and thus its significance to *The Flowering of the Rod*:

> Church Street was our street, the Church was our Church. It was founded by Count Zinzendorf who named our town Bethlehem.

People tell one things, and other children laugh at one's ignorance. "But Jesus was not born *here*."

That may be true. We will not discuss the matter. Only after some forty years, we approach it. "I don't know if I dreamed this or if I just imagined it, or if later I imagined that I dreamed it." "It does not matter," [Freud] said, "whether you dreamed it or imagined it or whether you just made it up, this moment. I do not think you would deliberately falsify your findings. The important thing is that it shows the trend of your fantasy or imagination."

He goes on, "You were born in Bethlehem? It is inevitable that the Christian myth—" he paused. "This does not offend you?" "Offend me?" "My speaking of your religion in terms of myth," he said. I said, "How could I be offended?" "Bethlehem is the town of Mary," he said.

Karnak and London and Bethlehem and Philadelphia had their histories, and "my mind (yours)", she wrote, "has its peculiar ego-centric personal approach to the eternal realities." With the proof sheets of *The Walls Do Not Fall*, H.D. played a little game, marking passages and initialling them for those to whom they seemed most appropriate. For herself she chose

> We are voyagers, discoverers
> of the not known.

She made the not-known known. Like Kaspar she brought myrrh to myrrh.

·Norman Holmes Pearson

New Haven
March 1973

CONTENTS

THE WALLS DO NOT FALL

To Bryher

for Karnak 1923
from London 1942

[1]

An incident here and there,
and rails gone (for guns)
from your (and my) old town square:

mist and mist-grey, no colour,
still the Luxor bee, chick and hare
pursue unalterable purpose

in green, rose-red, lapis;
they continue to prophesy
from the stone papyrus:

there, as here, ruin opens
the tomb, the temple; enter,
there as here, there are no doors:

the shrine lies open to the sky,
the rain falls, here, there
sand drifts; eternity endures:

ruin everywhere, yet as the fallen roof
leaves the sealed room
open to the air,

so, through our desolation,
thoughts stir, inspiration stalks us
through gloom:

unaware, Spirit announces the Presence;
shivering overtakes us,
as of old, Samuel:

3

*Luxor –
city in
Egypt.
Site of
Thebes.

Destruction of
present placed alongside
the fragmented survival
of the past; emphasis
on symbols, which
speak across time
and cultures, reminds
us of our reliance
on language and
the vital role of
language in the work
of the poet.
Communication has
become her responsibility
as a war time
poet.

temple, shrine, sealed
room evoking past,
but contrasting the old
town square – 'sealed'
physical space –
Contrast to
'rails gone'

trembling at a known street-corner,
we know not nor are known;
the Pythian pronounces—we pass on

to another cellar, to another sliced wall
where poor utensils show
like rare objects in a museum;

in museums / there are utensils / from past cultures

Pompeii has nothing to teach us,
we know crack of volcanic fissure,
slow flow of terrible lava,

pressure on heart, lungs, the brain
about to burst its brittle case
(what the skull can endure!):

Apocolyptical.

over us, Apocryphal fire,
under us, the earth sway, dip of a floor,
slope of a pavement

where men roll, drunk
with a new bewilderment,
sorcery, bedevilment:

the bone-frame was made for
no such shock knit within terror,
yet the skeleton stood up to it:

the flesh? it was melted away,
the heart burnt out, dead ember,
tendons, muscles shattered, outer husk dismembered

yet the frame held:
we passed the flame: we wonder
what saved us? what for?

4

Evil was active in the land,
Good was impoverished and sad;

Ill promised adventure,
Good was smug and fat;

Dev-ill was after us,
tricked up like Jehovah;

Good was the tasteless pod,
stripped from the manna-beans, pulse, lentils:

they were angry when we were so hungry
for the nourishment, God;

they snatched off our amulets,
charms are not, they said, grace;

but gods always face two-ways,
so let us search the old highways

for the true-rune, the right-spell,
recover old values;

nor listen if they shout out,
your beauty, Isis, Aset or Astarte,

is a harlot; you are retrogressive,
zealot, hankering after old flesh-pots;

your heart, moreover,
is a dead canker,

they continue, and
your rhythm is the devil's hymn,

your stylus is dipped in corrosive sublimate,
how can you scratch out

indelible ink of the palimpsest
of past misadventure?

Let us, however, recover the Sceptre,
the rod of power:

it is crowned with the lily-head
or the lily-bud:

it is Caduceus; among the dying
it bears healing:

or evoking the dead,
it brings life to the living.

[4]

There is a spell, for instance,
in every sea-shell:

continuous, the sea thrust
is powerless against coral,

bone, stone, marble
hewn from within by that craftsman,

the shell-fish:
oyster, clam, mollusc

is master-mason planning
the stone marvel:

yet that flabby, amorphous hermit
within, like the planet

senses the finite,
it limits its orbit

of being, its house,
temple, fane, shrine:

it unlocks the portals
at stated intervals:

prompted by hunger,
it opens to the tide-flow:

but infinity? no,
of nothing-too-much:

8

I sense my own limit,
my shell-jaws snap shut

at invasion of the limitless,
ocean-weight; infinite water

can not crack me, egg in egg-shell;
closed in, complete, immortal

full-circle, I know the pull
of the tide, the lull

as well as the moon;
the octopus-darkness

is powerless against
her cold immortality;

so I in my own way know
that the whale ——— *reference to Jonah?*

can not digest me:
be firm in your own small, static, limited

orbit and the shark-jaws
of outer circumstance

will spit you forth:
be indigestible, hard, ungiving *?*

so that, living within,
you beget, self-out-of-self,

selfless,
that pearl-of-great-price.

When in the company of the gods,
I loved and was loved,

never was my mind stirred
to such rapture,

my heart moved
to such pleasure,

as now, to discover
over Love, a new Master:

His, the track in the sand
from a plum-tree in flower

to a half-open hut-door,
(or track would have been

but wind blows sand-prints from the sand,
whether seen or unseen):

His, the Genius in the jar
which the Fisherman finds,

He is Mage,
bringing myrrh.

[6]

In me (the worm) clearly
is no righteousness, but this—

persistence; I escaped spider-snare,
bird-claw, scavenger bird-beak,

clung to grass-blade,
the back of a leaf

when storm-wind
tore it from its stem;

I escaped, I explored
rose-thorn forest,

was rain-swept
down the valley of a leaf;

was deposited on grass,
where mast by jewelled mast

bore separate ravellings
of encrusted gem-stuff

of the mist
from each banner-staff:

unintimidated by multiplicity
of magnified beauty,

such as your gorgon-great
dull eye can not focus

nor compass, I profit
by every calamity;

I eat my way out of it;
gorged on vine-leaf and mulberry,

parasite, I find nourishment:
when you cry in disgust,

a worm on the leaf,
a worm in the dust,

a worm on the ear-of-wheat,
I am yet unrepentant,

for I know how the Lord God
is about to manifest, when I,

the industrious worm,
spin my own shroud.

[7]

Gods, goddesses
wear the winged head-dress

of horns, as the butterfly
antennae,

or the erect king-cobra crest
to show how the worm turns.

[8]

So we reveal our status
with twin-horns, disk, erect serpent,

though these or the double-plume or lotus
are, you now tell us, trivial

intellectual adornment;
poets are useless,

more than that,
we, authentic relic,

bearers of the secret wisdom,
living remnant

of the inner band
of the sanctuaries' initiate,

are not only 'non-utilitarian',
we are 'pathetic':

this is the new heresy;
but if you do not even understand what words say,

how can you expect to pass judgement
on what words conceal?

yet the ancient rubrics reveal that
we are back at the beginning:

you have a long way to go,
walk carefully, speak politely

to those who have done their worm-cycle,
for gods have been smashed before

and idols and their secret is stored
in man's very speech,

in the trivial or
the real dream; insignia

in the heron's crest,
the asp's back,

enigmas, rubrics promise as before,
protection for the scribe;

he takes precedence of the priest,
stands second only to the Pharoah.

Thoth, Hermes, the stylus,
the palette, the pen, the quill endure,

though our books are a floor
of smouldering ash under our feet;

though the burning of the books remains
the most perverse gesture

and the meanest
of man's mean nature,

yet give us, they still cry,
give us books,

folio, manuscript, old parchment
will do for cartridge cases;

irony is bitter truth
wrapped up in a little joke,

and Hatshepsut's name is still circled
with what they call the *cartouche*.

[10]

But we fight for life,
we fight, they say, for breath,

so what good are your scribblings?
this—we take them with us

beyond death; Mercury, Hermes, Thoth
invented the script, letters, palette;

the indicated flute or lyre-notes
on papyrus or parchment

are magic, indelibly stamped
on the atmosphere somewhere,

forever; remember, O Sword,
you are the younger brother, the latter-born,

your Triumph, however exultant,
must one day be over,

in the beginning
was the Word.

Without thought, invention,
you would not have been, O Sword,

without idea and the Word's mediation,
you would have remained

unmanifest in the dim dimension
where thought dwells,

and beyond thought and idea,
their begetter,

Dream,
Vision.

So, in our secretive, sly way,
we are proud and chary

of companionship with you others,
our betters, who seem to imply

that we will soon be swept aside,
crumpled rags, no good for banner-stuff,

no fit length for a bandage;
but when the shingles hissed

in the rain of incendiary,
other values were revealed to us,

other standards hallowed us;
strange texture, a wing covered us,

and though there was whirr and roar in the high air,
there was a Voice louder,

though its speech was lower
than a whisper.

[13]

The Presence was spectrum-blue,
ultimate blue ray,

rare as radium, as healing;
my old self, wrapped round me,

was shroud (I speak of myself individually
but I was surrounded by companions

in this mystery);
do you wonder we are proud,

aloof,
indifferent to your good and evil?

peril, strangely encountered, strangely endured,
marks us;

we know each other
by secret symbols,

though, remote, speechless,
we pass each other on the pavement,

at the turn of the stair;
though no word pass between us,

there is subtle appraisement;
even if we snarl a brief greeting

20

or do not speak at all,
we know our Name,

we nameless initiates,
born of one mother,

companions
of the flame.

[14]

Yet we, the latter-day twice-born,
have our bad moments when

dragging the forlorn
husk of self after us,

we are forced to confess to
malaise and embarrassment;

we pull at this dead shell,
struggle but we must wait

till the new Sun dries off
the old-body humours;

awkwardly, we drag this stale
old will, old volition, old habit

about with us;
we are these people,

wistful, ironical, wilful,
who have no part in

new-world reconstruction,
in the confederacy of labour,

the practical issues of art
and the cataloguing of utilities:

O, do not look up
into the air,

you who are occupied
in the bewildering

sand-heap maze
of present-day endeavour;

you will be, not so much frightened
as paralysed with inaction,

and anyhow,
we have not crawled so very far

up our individual grass-blade
toward our individual star.

Too old to be useful
(whether in years or experience,

we are the same lot)
not old enough to be dead,

we are the keepers of the secret,
the carriers, the spinners

of the rare intangible thread
that binds all humanity

to ancient wisdom,
to antiquity;

our joy is unique, to us,
grape, knife, cup, wheat

are symbols in eternity,
and every concrete object

has abstract value, is timeless
in the dream parallel

whose relative sigil has not changed
since Nineveh and Babel.

Ra, Osiris, *Amen* appeared
in a spacious, bare meeting-house;

he is the world-father,
father of past aeons,

present and future equally;
beardless, not at all like Jehovah,

he was upright, slender,
impressive as the Memnon monolith,

yet he was not out of place
but perfectly at home

in that eighteenth-century
simplicity and grace;

then I woke with a start
of wonder and asked myself,

but whose eyes are those eyes?
for the eyes (in the cold,

I marvel to remember)
were all one texture,

as if without pupil
or all pupil, dark

yet very clear with amber
shining . . .

25

. . . coals for the world's burning,
for we must go forward,

we are at the cross-roads,
the tide is turning;

it uncovers pebbles and shells,
beautiful yet static, empty

old thought, old convention;
let us go down to the sea,

gather dry sea-weed,
heap drift-wood,

let us light a new fire
and in the fragrance

of burnt salt and sea-incense
chant new paeans to the new Sun

of regeneration;
we have always worshipped Him,

we have always said,
forever and ever, Amen.

The Christos-image
is most difficult to disentangle

from its art-craft junk-shop
paint-and-plaster medieval jumble

of pain-worship and death-symbol,
that is why, I suppose, the Dream

deftly stage-managed the bare, clean
early colonial interior,

without stained-glass, picture,
image or colour,

for now it appears obvious
that *Amen* is our Christos.

He might even be the authentic Jew
stepped out from Velasquez;

those eye-lids in the Velasquez
are lowered over eyes

that open, would daze, bewilder
and stun us with the old sense of guilt

and fear, but the terror of those eyes
veiled in their agony is over;

I assure you that the eyes
of Velasquez' crucified

now look straight at you,
and they are amber and they are fire.

Now it appears very clear
that the Holy Ghost,

childhood's mysterious enigma,
is the Dream;

that way of inspiration
is always open,

and open to everyone;
it acts as go-between, interpreter,

it explains symbols of the past
in to-day's imagery,

it merges the distant future
with most distant antiquity,

states economically
in a simple dream-equation

the most profound philosophy,
discloses the alchemist's secret

and follows the Mage
in the desert.

Splintered the crystal of identity,
shattered the vessel of integrity,

till the Lord *Amen*,
paw-er of the ground,

bearer of the curled horns,
bellows from the horizon:

here am I, Amen-Ra,
Amen, Aries, the Ram;

time, time for you to begin a new spiral,
see—I toss you into the star-whirlpool;

till pitying, pitying,
snuffing the ground,

here am I, Amen-Ra whispers,
Amen, Aries, the Ram,

be cocoon, smothered in wool,
be Lamb, mothered again.

Now my right hand,
now my left hand

clutch your curled fleece;
take me home, take me home,

my voice wails from the ground;
take me home, Father:

pale as the worm in the grass,
yet I am a spark

struck by your hoof from a rock:
Amen, you are so warm,

hide me in your fleece,
crop me up with the new-grass;

let your teeth devour me,
let me be warm in your belly,

the sun-disk,
the re-born Sun.

[23]

Take me home
where canals

flow
between iris-banks:

where the heron
has her nest:

where the mantis
prays on the river-reed:

where the grasshopper says
Amen, Amen, Amen.

Or anywhere
where stars blaze through clear air,

where we may greet individually,
Sirius, Vega, Arcturus,

where these separate entities
are intimately concerned with us,

where each, with its particular attribute,
may be invoked

with accurate charm, spell, prayer,
which will reveal unquestionably,

whatever healing or inspirational essence
is necessary for whatever particular ill

the inquiring soul is heir to:
O stars, little jars of that indisputable

and absolute Healer, Apothecary,
wrought, faceted, jewelled

boxes, very precious, to hold further
unguent, myrrh, incense:

jasper, beryl, sapphire
that, as we draw them nearer

by prayer, spell,
litany, incantation,

will reveal their individual fragrance,
personal magnetic influence,

become, as they once were,
personified messengers,

healers, helpers
of the One, *Amen*, All-father.

[25]

Amen,
only just now,

my heart-shell
breaks open,

though long ago, the phoenix,
your *bennu* bird

dropped a grain,
as of scalding wax;

there was fragrance, burnt incense,
myrtle, aloes, cedar;

the Kingdom is a Tree
whose roots bind the heart-husk

to earth,
after the ultimate grain,

lodged in the heart-core,
has taken its nourishment.

[26]

What fruit is our store,
what flower?

what savour do we possess,
what particular healing-of-the-nations

is our leaf? is it balsomodendron,
herb-basil, or is ours

the spear and leaf-spire
of the palm?

are we born from island or oasis
or do we stand

fruit-less on the field-edge,
to spread

shade to the wheat-gatherers
in the noon-heat?

Is ours lotus-tree
from the lotus-grove,

magnolia's heavy, heady, sleepy
dream?

or pomegranate
whose name decorates sonnets,

but either acid or over-ripe,
perfect only for the moment?

of all the flowering of the wood,
are we wild-almond, winter-cherry?

or are we pine or fir,
sentinel, solitary?

or cypress,
arbutus-fragrant?

O Heart, small urn
of porphyry, agate or cornelian,

how imperceptibly the grain fell
between a heart-beat of pleasure

and a heart-beat of pain;
I do not know how it came

nor how long it had lain there,
nor can I say

how it escaped tempest
of passion and malice,

nor why it was not washed away
in flood of sorrow,

or dried up in the bleak drought
of bitter thought.

Grant us strength to endure
a little longer,

now the heart's alabaster
is broken;

we would feed forever
on the amber honey-comb

of your remembered greeting,
but the old-self,

still half at-home in the world,
cries out in anger,

I am hungry, the children cry for food
and flaming stones fall on them;

our awareness leaves us defenceless;
O, for your Presence

among the fishing-nets
by the beached boats on the lake-edge;

when, in the drift of wood-smoke,
will you say again, as you said,

the baked fish is ready,
here is the bread?

[30]

I heard Scorpion whet his knife,
I feared Archer (taut his bow),

Goat's horns were threat,
would climb high? then fall low;

across the abyss
the Waterman waited,

this is the age of the new dimension,
dare, seek, seek further, dare more,

here is the alchemist's key,
it unlocks secret doors,

the present goes a step further
toward fine distillation of emótion,

the elixir of life, the philosopher's stone
is yours if you surrender

sterile logic, trivial reason;
so mind dispersed, dared occult lore,

found secret doors unlocked,
floundered, was lost in sea-depth,

sub-conscious ocean where Fish
move two-ways, devour;

40

when identity in the depth,
would merge with the best,

octopus or shark rise
from the sea-floor:

illusion, reversion of old values,
oneness lost, madness.

[31]

Wistfulness, exaltation,
a pure core of burning cerebration,

jottings on a margin,
indecipherable palimpsest scribbled over

with too many contradictory emotions,
search for finite definition

of the infinite, stumbling toward
vague cosmic expression,

obvious sentiment,
folder round a spiritual bank-account,

with credit-loss too starkly indicated,
a riot of unpruned imagination,

jottings of psychic numerical equations,
runes, superstitions, evasions,

invasion of the over-soul into a cup
too brittle, a jar too circumscribed,

a little too porous to contain the out-flowing
of water-about-to-be-changed-to-wine

at the wedding; barren search,
arrogance, over-confidence, pitiful reticence,

42

boasting, intrusion of strained
inappropriate allusion,

illusion of lost-gods, daemons;
gambler with eternity,

initiate of the secret wisdom,
bride of the kingdom,

reversion of old values,
oneness lost, madness.

Depth of the sub-conscious spews forth
too many incongruent monsters

and fixed indigestible matter
such as shell, pearl; imagery

done to death; perilous ascent,
ridiculous descent; rhyme, jingle,

overworked assonance, nonsense,
juxtaposition of words for words' sake,

without meaning, undefined; imposition,
deception, indecisive weather-vane;

disagreeable, inconsequent syllables,
too malleable, too brittle,

over-sensitive, under-definitive,
clash of opposites, fight of emotion

and sterile invention—
you find all this?

conditioned to the discrimination
of the colours of the lunar rainbow

and the outer layers of the feathers
of the butterfly's antennae,

we were caught up by the tornado
and deposited on no pleasant ground,

but we found the angle of incidence
equals the angle of reflection;

separated from the wandering stars
and the habits of the lordly fixed ones,

we noted that even the erratic burnt-out comet
has its peculiar orbit.

[33]

Let us measure defeat
in terms of bread and meat,

and continents
in relative extent of wheat

fields; let us not teach
what we have learned badly

and not profited by;
let us not concoct

healing potions for the dead,
nor invent

new colours
for blind eyes.

We have seen how the most amiable,
under physical stress,

become wolves, jackals,
mongrel curs;

we know further that hunger
may make hyenas of the best of us;

let us, therefore (though we do not forget
Love, the Creator,

her chariot and white doves),
entreat Hest,

Aset, Isis, the great enchantress,
in her attribute of Serqet,

the original great-mother,
who drove

harnessed scorpions
before her.

Let us substitute
enchantment for sentiment,

re-dedicate our gifts
to spiritual realism,

scrape a palette,
point pen or brush,

prepare papyrus or parchment,
offer incense to Thoth,

the original Ancient-of-days,
Hermes-thrice-great,

let us entreat
that he, by his tau-cross,

invoke the true-magic,
lead us back to the one-truth,

let him (Wisdom),
in the light of what went before,

illuminate what came after,
re-vivify the eternal verity,

be ye wise
as asps, scorpions, *as serpents.*

[36]

In no wise is the pillar-of-fire
that went before

different from the pillar-of-fire
that comes after;

chasm, schism in consciousness
must be bridged over;

we are each, householder,
each with a treasure;

now is the time to re-value
our secret hoard

in the light of both past and future,
for whether

coins, gems, gold
beakers, platters,

or merely
talismans, records or parchments,

explicitly, we are told,
it contains

*for every scribe
which is instructed,*

*things new
and old.*

49

[37]

Thou shalt have none other gods but me;
not on the sea

shall we entreat Triton or Dolphin,
not on the land

shall we lift rapt face and clasp hands
before laurel or oak-tree,

not in the sky
shall we invoke separately

Orion or Sirius
or the followers of the Bear,

not in the higher air
of Algorab, Regulus or Deneb

shall we cry
for help—or shall we?

This search for historical parallels,
research into psychic affinities,

has been done to death before,
will be done again;

no comment can alter spiritual realities
(you say) or again,

what new light can you possibly
throw upon them?

my mind (yours),
your way of thought (mine),

each has its peculiar intricate map,
threads weave over and under

the jungle-growth
of biological aptitudes,

inherited tendencies,
the intellectual effort

of the whole race,
its tide and ebb;

but my mind (yours)
has its peculiar ego-centric

personal approach
to the eternal realities,

and differs from every other
in minute particulars,

as the vein-paths on any leaf
differ from those of every other leaf

in the forest, as every snow-flake
has its particular star, coral or prism shape.

[39]

We have had too much consecration,
too little affirmation,

too much: but this, this, this
has been proved heretical,

too little: I know, I feel
the meaning that words hide;

they are anagrams, cryptograms,
little boxes, conditioned

to hatch butterflies . . .

For example:
Osiris equates O-sir-is or O-Sire-is;

Osiris,
the star Sirius,

relates resurrection myth
and resurrection reality

through the ages;
plasterer, crude mason,

not too well equipped, my thought
would cover deplorable gaps

in time, reveal the regrettable chasm,
bridge that before-and-after schism,

(before Abraham was I am)
uncover cankerous growths

in present-day philosophy,
in an endeavour to make ready,

as it were, the patient for the Healer;
correlate faith with faith,

recover the secret of Isis,
which is: there was One

in the beginning, Creator,
Fosterer, Begetter, the Same-forever

in the papyrus-swamp
in the Judean meadow.

Sirius:
what mystery is this?

you are seed,
corn near the sand,
enclosed in black-lead,
ploughed land.

Sirius:
what mystery is this?

you are drowned
in the river;
the spring freshets
push open the water-gates.

Sirius:
what mystery is this?

where heat breaks and cracks
the sand-waste,
you are a mist
of snow: white, little flowers.

O, Sire, is this the path?
over sedge, over dune-grass,

silently
sledge-runners pass.

O, Sire, is this the waste?
unbelievably,

sand glistens like ice,
cold, cold;

drawn to the temple-gate, O, Sire,
is this union at last?

Still the walls do not fall,
I do not know why;

there is zrr-hiss,
lightning in a not-known,

unregistered dimension;
we are powerless,

dust and powder fill our lungs
our bodies blunder

through doors twisted on hinges,
and the lintels slant

cross-wise;
we walk continually

on thin air
that thickens to a blind fog,

then step swiftly aside,
for even the air

is independable,
thick where it should be fine

and tenuous
where wings separate and open,

and the ether
is heavier than the floor,

and the floor sags
like a ship floundering;

we know no rule
of procedure,

we are voyagers, discoverers
of the not-known,

the unrecorded;
we have no map;

possibly we will reach haven,
heaven.

TRIBUTE TO THE ANGELS

To Osbert Sitwell

. . . possibly we will reach haven,
heaven.

Hermes Trismegistus
is patron of alchemists;

his province is thought,
inventive, artful and curious;

his metal is quicksilver,
his clients, orators, thieves and poets;

steal then, O orator,
plunder, O poet,

take what the old-church
found in Mithra's tomb,

candle and script and bell,
take what the new-church spat upon

and broke and shattered;
collect the fragments of the splintered glass

and of your fire and breath,
melt down and integrate,

re-invoke, re-create
opal, onyx, obsidian,

now scattered in the shards
men tread upon.

Your walls do not fall, he said,
because your walls are made of jasper;

but not four-square, I thought,
another shape (octahedron?)

slipped into the place
reserved by rule and rite

for the *twelve foundations*,
for the *transparent glass*,

for *no need of the sun*
nor *moon to shine*;

for the vision as we see
or have seen or imagined it

or in the past invoked
or conjured up or had conjured

by another, was usurped;
I saw the shape

which might have been of jasper,
but it was not four-square.

[3]

I John saw. I testify;
if any man shall add

God shall add unto him the plagues,
but he that sat upon the throne said,

I make all things new.
I John saw. I testify,

but *I make all things new,*
said He of the seven stars,

he of the seventy-times-seven
passionate, bitter wrongs,

He of the seventy-times-seven
bitter, unending wars.

[4]

Not in our time, O Lord,
the plowshare for the sword,

not in our time, the knife,
sated with life-blood and life,

to trim the barren vine;
no grape-leaf for the thorn,

no vine-flower for the crown;
not in our time, O King,

the voice to quell the re-gathering,
thundering storm.

[5]

Nay—*peace be still*—
lovest thou not Azrael,

the last and greatest, Death?
lovest not the sun,

the first who giveth life,
Raphael? *lovest thou me?*

lover of sand and shell,
know who withdraws the veil,

holds back the tide and shapes
shells to the wave-shapes? Gabriel:

Raphael, Gabriel, Azrael,   *Azrael is not*
three of seven—what is War   *1 of 7...*

to Birth, to Change, to Death?
yet he, red-fire is one of seven fires,

judgement and will of God,
God's very breath—Uriel. — *Summer?*

67

Never in Rome,
so many martyrs fell;

not in Jerusalem,
never in Thebes,

so many stood and watched
chariot-wheels turning,

saw with their very eyes,
the battle of the Titans,

saw Zeus' thunderbolts in action
and how from giant hands,

the lightning shattered earth
and splintered sky, nor fled

to hide in caves,
but with unbroken will,

with unbowed head, watched
and though unaware, worshipped

and knew not that they worshipped
and that they were

that which they worshipped,
had they known the fire

of strength, endurance, anger
in their hearts,

was part of that same fire
that in a candle on a candle-stick

or in a star,
is known as one of seven,

is named among the seven Angels,
Uriel.

[7]

To Uriel, no shrine, no temple
where the red-death fell,

no image by the city-gate,
no torch to shine across the water,

no new fane in the market-place:
the lane is empty but the levelled wall

is purple as with purple spread
upon an altar,

this is the flowering of the rood,
this is the flowering of the reed,

where, Uriel, we pause to give
thanks that we rise again from death and live

70

[8]

Now polish the crucible
and in the bowl distill

a word most bitter, *marah*,
a word bitterer still, *mar*,

sea, brine, breaker, seducer,
giver of life, giver of tears;

Now polish the crucible
and set the jet of flame

under, till *marah-mar*
are melted, fuse and join

and change and alter,
mer, mere, mère, mater, Maia, Mary,

Gener for mother

Star of the Sea,
Mother.

Rebirth.

[9]

Bitter, bitter jewel
in the heart of the bowl,

what is your colour?
what do you offer

to us who rebel?
what were we had you loved other?

what is this mother-father
to tear at our entrails?

what is this unsatisfied duality
which you can not satisfy?

In the field-furrow
the rain-water

showed splintered edge
as of a broken mirror,

and in the glass
as in a polished spear,

glowed the star Hesperus,
white, far and luminous,

incandescent and near,
Venus, Aphrodite, Astarte,

star of the east,
star of the west,

Phosphorus at sun-rise,
Hesperus at sun-set.

O swiftly, re-light the flame
before the substance cool,

for suddenly we saw your name
desecrated; knaves and fools

have done you impious wrong,
Venus, for venery stands for impurity

and Venus as desire
is venereous, lascivious,

while the very root of the word shrieks
like a mandrake when foul witches pull

its stem at midnight,
and rare mandragora itself

is full, they say, of poison,
food for the witches' den.

Swiftly re-light the flame,
Aphrodite, holy name,

Astarte, hull and spar
of wrecked ships lost your star,

forgot the light at dusk,
forgot the prayer at dawn;

return, O holiest one,
Venus whose name is kin

to venerate,
venerator.

"What is the jewel colour?"
green-white, opalescent,

with under-layer of changing blue,
with rose-vein; a white agate

with a pulse uncooled that beats yet,
faint blue-violet;

it lives, it breathes,
it gives off—fragrance?

I do not know what it gives,
a vibration that we can not name

for there is no name for it;
my patron said, "name it";

I said, I can not name it,
there is no name;

he said,
"invent it".

I can not invent it,
I said it was agate,

I said, it lived, it gave—
fragrance—was near enough

to explain that quality
for which there is no name;

I do not want to name it,
I want to watch its faint

heart-beat, pulse-beat
as it quivers, I do not want

to talk about it,
I want to minimize thought,

concentrate on it
till I shrink,

dematerialize
and am drawn into it.

Annael—this was another voice,
hardly a voice, a breath, a whisper,

and I remembered bell-notes,
Azrael, Gabriel, Raphael,

as when in Venice, one of the campanili
speaks and another answers,

until it seems the whole city (Venice-Venus)
will be covered with gold pollen shaken

from the bell-towers, lilies plundered
with the weight of massive bees . . .

Annael—and I remembered the sea-shell
and I remembered the empty lane

and I thought again of people,
daring the blinding rage

of the lightning, and I thought,
there is no shrine, no temple

in the city for that other, *Uriel*,
and I knew his companion,

companion of the fire-to-endure
was another fire, another candle,

was another of seven,
named among the seven Angels,

Annael,
peace of God.

So we hail them together,
one to contrast the other,

two of the seven Spirits,
set before God

as lamps on the high-altar,
for one must inexorably

take fire from the other
as spring from winter,

and surely never, never
was a spring more bountiful

than this; never, never
was a season more beautiful,

richer in leaf and colour;
tell me, in what other place

will you find the may flowering
mulberry and rose-purple?

tell me, in what other city
will you find the may-tree

so delicate, green-white, opalescent
like our jewel in the crucible?

For Uriel, no temple
but everywhere,

the outer precincts and the squares
are fragrant;

the festival opens as before
with the dove's murmuring;

for Uriel, no temple
but Love's sacred groves,

withered in Thebes and Tyre,
flower elsewhere.

[19]

We see her visible and actual,
beauty incarnate,

as no high-priest of Astoroth
could compel her

with incense
and potent spell;

we asked for no sign
but she gave a sign unto us;

sealed with the seal of death,
we thought not to entreat her

but prepared us for burial;
then she set a charred tree before us,

burnt and stricken to the heart;
was it may-tree or apple?

Invisible, indivisible Spirit,
how is it you come so near,

how is it that we dare
approach the high-altar?

we crossed the charred portico,
passed through a frame—doorless—

entered a shrine; like a ghost,
we entered a house through a wall;

then still not knowing
whether (like the wall)

we were there or not-there,
we saw the tree flowering;

it was an ordinary tree
in an old garden-square.

This is no rune nor riddle,
it is happening everywhere;

what I mean is—it is so simple
yet no trick of the pen or brush

could capture that impression;
music could do nothing with it,

nothing whatever; what I mean is—
but you have seen for yourself

that burnt-out wood crumbling . . .
you have seen for yourself.

A new sensation
is not granted to everyone,

not to everyone everywhere,
but to us here, a new sensation

strikes paralysing,
strikes dumb,

strikes the senses numb,
sets the nerves quivering;

I am sure you see
what I mean;

it was an old tree
such as we see everywhere,

anywhere here—and some barrel staves
and some bricks

and an edge of the wall
uncovered and the naked ugliness

and then . . . music? O, what I meant
by music when I said music, was—

music sets up ladders,
it makes us invisible,

it sets us apart,
it lets us escape;

but from the visible
there is no escape;

there is no escape from the spear
that pierces the heart.

We are part of it;
we admit the transubstantiation,

not God merely in bread
but God in the other-half of the tree

that looked dead—
did I bow my head?

did I weep? my eyes saw,
it was not a dream

yet it was vision,
it was a sign,

it was *the Angel which redeemed me,*
it was the Holy Ghost—

a half-burnt-out apple-tree
blossoming;

this is the flowering of the rood,
this is the flowering of the wood

where Annael, we pause to give
thanks that we rise again from death and live.

[24]

Every hour, every moment
has its specific attendant Spirit;

the clock-hand, minute by minute,
ticks round its prescribed orbit;

but this curious mechanical perfection
should not separate but relate rather,

our life, this temporary eclipse
to that other . . .

. . . of the *no need*
of the moon to shine in it,

for it was ticking minute by minute
(the clock at my bed-head,

with its dim, luminous disc)
when the Lady knocked;

I was talking casually
with friends in the other room,

when we saw the outer hall
grow lighter—then we saw where the door was,

there was no door
(this was a dream of course),

and she was standing there,
actually, at the turn of the stair.

One of us said, how odd,
she is actually standing there,

I wonder what brought her?
another of us said,

have we some power between us,
we three together,

that acts as a sort of magnet,
that attracts the super-natural?

(yet it was all natural enough,
we agreed);

I do not know what I said
or if I said anything,

for before I had time to speak,
I realized I had been dreaming,

that I lay awake now on my bed,
that the luminous light

was the phosphorescent face
of my little clock

and the faint knocking
was the clock ticking.

[27]

And yet in some very subtle way,
she was there more than ever,

as if she had mira   lously
related herself to   ne here,

which is no easy   ick, difficult
even for the ex   ienced stranger,

of whom we n   st *be not forgetful*
for *some have e   rtained angels unawares.*

I had been thinking of Gabriel,
of the moon-cycle, of the moon-shell,

of the moon-crescent
and the moon at full:

I had been thinking of Gabriel,
the moon-regent, the Angel,

and I had intended to recall him
in the sequence of candle and fire

and the law of the seven;
I had not forgotten

his special attribute
of annunciator; I had thought

to address him as I had the others,
Uriel, Annael;

how could I imagine
the Lady herself would come instead?

We have seen her
the world over,

Our Lady of the Goldfinch,
Our Lady of the Candelabra,

Our Lady of the Pomegranate,
Our Lady of the Chair;

we have seen her, an empress,
magnificent in pomp and grace,

and we have seen her
with a single flower

or a cluster of garden-pinks
in a glass beside her;

we have seen her snood
drawn over her hair,

or her face set in profile
with the blue hood and stars;

we have seen her head bowed down
with the weight of a domed crown,

or we have seen her, a wisp of a girl
trapped in a golden halo;

we have seen her with arrow, with doves
and a heart like a valentine;

we have seen her in fine silks imported
from all over the Levant,

and hung with pearls brought
from the city of Constantine;

we have seen her sleeve
of every imaginable shade

of damask and figured brocade;
it is true,

the painters did very well by her;
it is true, they missed never a line

of the suave turn of the head
or subtle shade of lowered eye-lid

or eye-lids half-raised; you find
her everywhere (or did find),

in cathedral, museum, cloister,
at the turn of the palace stair.

We see her hand in her lap,
smoothing the apple-green

or the apple-russet silk;
we see her hand at her throat,

fingering a talisman
brought by a crusader from Jerusalem;

we see her hand unknot a Syrian veil
or lay down a Venetian shawl

on a polished table that reflects
half a miniature broken column;

we see her stare past a mirror
through an open window,

where boat follows slow boat on the lagoon;
there are white flowers on the water.

[31]

But none of these, none of these
suggest her as I saw her,

though we approach possibly
something of her cool beneficence

in the gracious friendliness
of the marble sea-maids in Venice,

who climb the altar-stair
at *Santa Maria dei Miracoli*,

or we acclaim her in the name
of another in Vienna,

Maria von dem Schnee,
Our Lady of the Snow.

For I can say truthfully,
her veils were *white as snow*,

so as no fuller on earth
can white them; I can say

she looked beautiful, she looked lovely,
she was *clothed with a garment*

down to the foot, but it was not
girt about with a golden girdle,

there was no gold, no colour
there was no gleam in the stuff

nor shadow of hem and seam,
as it fell to the floor; she bore

none of her usual attributes;
the Child was not with her.

[33]

Hermes took his attribute
of Leader-of-the-dead from Thoth

and the T-cross becomes caduceus;
the old-church makes its invocation

to Saint Michael and Our Lady
at the death-bed; Hermes Trismegistus

spears, with Saint Michael,
the darkness of ignorance,

casts the Old Dragon
into the abyss.

So Saint Michael,
regent of the planet Mercury,

is not absent
when we summon the other Angels,

another candle appears
on the high-altar,

it burns with a potent flame
but quivers

and quickens and darkens
and quickens again;

remember, it was Thoth
with a feather

who weighed the souls
of the dead.

So she must have been pleased with us,
who did not forgo our heritage

at the grave-edge;
she must have been pleased

with the straggling company of the brush and quill
who did not deny their birthright;

she must have been pleased with us,
for she looked so kindly at us

under her drift of veils,
and she carried a book.

[36]

Ah (you say), this is Holy Wisdom,
Santa Sophia, the SS of the *Sanctus Spiritus*,

so by facile reasoning, logically
the incarnate symbol of the Holy Ghost;

your Holy Ghost was an apple-tree
smouldering—or rather now bourgeoning

with flowers; the fruit of the Tree?
this is the new Eve who comes

clearly to return, to retrieve
what she lost the race,

given over to sin, to death;
she brings the Book of Life, obviously.

This is a symbol of beauty (you continue),
she is Our Lady universally,

I see her as you project her,
not out of place

flanked by Corinthian capitals,
or in a Coptic nave,

or frozen above the centre door
of a Gothic cathedral;

you have done very well by her
(to repeat your own phrase),

you have carved her tall and unmistakable,
a hieratic figure, the veiled Goddess,

whether of the seven delights,
whether of the seven spear-points.

O yes—you understand, I say,
this is all most satisfactory,

but she wasn't hieratic, she wasn't frozen,
she wasn't very tall;

she is the Vestal
from the days of Numa,

she carries over the cult
of the *Bona Dea*,

she carries a book but it is not
the tome of the ancient wisdom,

the pages, I imagine, are the blank pages
of the unwritten volume of the new;

all you say, is implicit,
all that and much more;

but she is not shut up in a cave
like a Sibyl; she is not

imprisoned in leaden bars
in a coloured window;

she is Psyche, the butterfly,
out of the cocoon.

But nearer than Guardian Angel
or good Daemon,

she is the counter-coin-side
of primitive terror;

she is not-fear, she is not-war,
but she is no symbolic figure

of peace, charity, chastity, goodness,
faith, hope, reward;

she is not Justice with eyes
blindfolded like Love's;

I grant you the dove's symbolic purity,
I grant you her face was innocent

and immaculate and her veils
like the Lamb's Bride,

but the Lamb was not with her,
either as Bridegroom or Child;

her attention is undivided,
we are her bridegroom and lamb;

her book is our book; written
or unwritten, its pages will reveal

a tale of a Fisherman,
a tale of a jar or jars,

the same—different—the same attributes,
different yet the same as before.

This is no rune nor symbol,
what I mean is—it is so simple

yet no trick of the pen or brush
could capture that impression;

what I wanted to indicate was
a new phase, a new distinction of colour;

I wanted to say, I did say
there was no sheen, no reflection,

no shadow; when I said white,
I did not mean sculptor's or painter's white,

nor porcelain; dim-white could
not suggest it, for when

is fresh-fallen snow (or snow
in the act of falling) dim?

yet even now, we stumble, we are lost—
what can we say?

she was not impalpable like a ghost,
she was not awe-inspiring like a Spirit,

she was not even over-whelming
like an Angel.

She carried a book, either to imply
she was one of us, with us,

or to suggest she was satisfied
with our purpose, a tribute to the Angels;

yet though the campanili spoke,
Gabriel, Azrael,

though the campanili answered,
Raphael, Uriel,

thought a distant note over-water
chimed *Annael*, and *Michael*

was implicit from the beginning,
another, deep, un-named, resurging bell

answered, sounding through them all:
remember, where there was

no need of the moon to shine . . .
I saw no temple.

Some call that deep-deep bell
Zadkiel, the righteousness of God,

he is regent of Jupiter
or Zeus-pater or Theus-pater,

Theus, God; God-the-father, father-god
or the Angel god-father,

himself, heaven yet at home in a star
whose colour is amethyst,

whose candle burns deep-violet
with the others.

[43]

And the point in the spectrum
where all lights become one,

is white and white is not no-colour,
as we were told as children,

but all-colour;
where the flames mingle

and the wings meet, when we gain
the arc of perfection,

we are satisfied, we are happy,
we begin again;

I John saw. I testify
to rainbow feathers, to the span of heaven

and walls of colour,
the colonnades of jasper;

but when the jewel
melts in the crucible,

we find not ashes, not ash-of-rose,
not a tall vase and a staff of lilies,

not *vas spirituale,*
not *rosa mystica* even,

but a cluster of garden-pinks
or a face like a Christmas-rose.

This is the flowering of the rod,
this is the flowering of the burnt-out wood,

where, Zadkiel, we pause to give
thanks that we rise again from death and live.

London
May 17-31, 1944.

THE FLOWERING OF THE ROD

To Norman Holmes Pearson

. . . pause to give
thanks that we rise again from death and live.

[1]

O the beautiful garment,
the beautiful raiment—

do not think of His face
or even His hands,

do not think how we will stand
before Him;

remember the snow
on Hermon;

do not look below
where the blue gentian

reflects geometric pattern
in the ice-floe;

do not be beguiled
by the geometry of perfection

for even now,
the terrible banner

darkens the bridge-head;
we have shown

that we could stand;
we have withstood

113

the anger, frustration,
bitter fire of destruction;

leave the smouldering cities below
(we have done all we could),

we have given until we have no more to give;
alas, it was pity, rather than love, we gave;

now having given all, let us leave all;
above all, let us leave pity

and mount higher
to love—resurrection.

I go where I love and where I am loved,
into the snow;

I go to the things I love
with no thought of duty or pity;

I go where I belong, inexorably,
as the rain that has lain long

in the furrow; I have given
or would have given

life to the grain;
but if it will not grow or ripen

with the rain of beauty,
the rain will return to the cloud;

the harvester sharpens his steel on the stone;
but this is not our field,

we have not sown this;
pitiless, pitiless, let us leave

The-place-of-a-skull
to those who have fashioned it.

In resurrection, there is confusion
if we start to argue; if we stand and stare,

we do not know where to go;
in resurrection, there is simple affirmation,

but do not delay to round up the others,
up and down the street; your going

in a moment like this, is the best proof
that you know the way;

does the first wild-goose stop to explain
to the others? no—he is off;

they follow or not
that is their affair;

does the first wild-goose care
whether the others follow or not?

I don't think so—he is so happy to be off—
he knows where he is going;

so we must be drawn or we must fly,
like the snow-geese of the Arctic circle,

to the Carolinas or to Florida,
or like those migratory flocks

who still (they say) hover
over the lost island, Atlantis;

seeking what we once knew,
we know ultimately we will find

happiness; *to-day shalt thou be
with me in Paradise.*

[4]

Blue-geese, white-geese, you may say,
yes, I know this duality, this double nostalgia;

I know the insatiable longing
in winter, for palm-shadow

and sand and burnt sea-drift;
but in the summer, as I watch

the wave till its edge of foam
touches the hot sand and instantly

vanishes like snow on the equator,
I would cry out, stay, stay;

then I remember delicate enduring frost
and its mid-winter dawn-pattern;

in the hot noon-sun, I think of the grey
opalescent winter-dawn; as the wave

burns on the shingle, I think,
you are less beautiful than frost;

but it is also true that I pray,
O, give me burning blue

and brittle burnt sea-weed
above the tide-line,

as I stand, still unsatisfied,
under the long shadow-on-snow of the pine.

[5]

Satisfied, unsatisfied,
satiated or numb with hunger,

this is the eternal urge,
this is the despair, the desire to equilibrate

the eternal variant;
you understand that insistent calling,

that demand of a given moment,
the will to enjoy, the will to live,

not merely the will to endure,
the will to flight, the will to achievement,

the will to rest after long flight;
but who knows the desperate urge

of those others—actual or perhaps now
mythical birds—who seek but find no rest

till they drop from the highest point of the spiral
or fall from the innermost centre of the ever-
        narrowing circle?

for they remember, they remember, as they sway
        and hover,
what once was—they remember, they remember—

they will not swerve—they have known bliss,
the fruit that satisfies—they have come back—

what if the islands are lost? what if the waters
cover the Hesperides? they would rather
    remember—

remember the golden apple-trees;
O, do not pity them, as you watch them drop
    one by one,

for they fall exhausted, numb, blind
but in certain ecstasy,

for theirs is the hunger
for Paradise.

[6]

So I would rather drown, remembering—
than bask on tropic atolls

in the coral-seas; I would rather drown
remembering—than rest on pine or fir-branch

where great stars pour down
their generating strength, Arcturus

or the sapphires of the Northern Crown;
I would rather beat in the wind, crying to these
    others:

yours is the more foolish circling,
yours is the senseless wheeling

round and round—yours has no reason—
I am seeking heaven;

yours has no vision,
I see what is beneath me, what is above me,

what men say is-not—I remember,
I remember, I remember—you have forgot:

you think, even before it is half-over,
that your cycle is at an end,

but you repeat your foolish circling—again,
    again, again;
again, the steel sharpened on the stone;

again, the pyramid of skulls;
I gave pity to the dead,

O blasphemy, pity is a stone for bread,
only love is holy and love's ecstasy

that turns and turns and turns about one centre,
reckless, regardless, blind to reality,

that knows the Islands of the Blest are there,
for *many waters can not quench love's fire.*

[7]

Yet resurrection is a sense of direction,
resurrection is a bee-line,

straight to the horde and plunder,
the treasure, the store-room,

the honeycomb;
resurrection is remuneration,

food, shelter, fragrance
of myrrh and balm.

[8]

I am so happy,
I am the first or the last

of a flock or a swarm;
I am *full of new wine;*

I am branded with a word,
I am burnt with wood,

drawn from glowing ember,
not cut, not marked with steel;

I am the first or the last to renounce
iron, steel, metal;

I have gone forward,
I have gone backward,

I have gone onward from bronze and iron,
into the Golden Age.

No poetic fantasy
but a biological reality,

a fact: I am an entity
like bird, insect, plant

or sea-plant cell;
I live; I am alive;

take care, do not know me,
deny me, do not recognise me,

shun me; for this reality
is infectious—ecstasy.

[10]

It is no madness to say
you will fall, you great cities,

(now the cities lie broken);
it is not tragedy, prophecy

from a frozen Priestess,
a lonely Pythoness

who chants, who sings
in broken hexameters,

doom, doom to city-gates,
to rulers, to kingdoms;

it is simple reckoning, algebraic,
it is geometry on the wing,

not patterned, a gentian
in an ice-mirror,

yet it is, if you like, a lily
folded like a pyramid,

a flower-cone,
not a heap of skulls;

it is a lily, if you will,
each petal, a kingdom, an aeon,

and it is the seed of a lily
that having flowered,

will flower again;
it is that smallest grain,

the least of all seeds
that grows branches

where the birds rest;
it is that flowering balm,

it is heal-all,
everlasting;

it is the greatest among herbs
and becometh a tree.

[11]

He was the first that flew
(the heavenly pointer)

but not content to leave
the scattered flock,

He journeys back and forth
between the poles of heaven and earth forever;

He was the first to wing
from that sad Tree,

but having flown, the Tree of Life
bears rose from thorn

and fragrant vine,
from barren wood;

He was the first to say,
not to the chosen few,

his faithful friends,
the wise and good,

but to an outcast and a vagabond,
to-day shalt thou be with me in Paradise.

So the first—it is written,
will be the twisted or the tortured individuals,

out of line, out of step with world so-called
     progress;
the first to receive the promise was a thief;

the first actually to witness His life-after-death,
was an unbalanced, neurotic woman,

who was naturally reviled for having left home
and not caring for house-work . . . or was that
     Mary of Bethany?

in any case—as to this other Mary
and what she did, everyone knows,

but it is not on record
exactly where and how she found the alabaster jar;

some say she took the house-money
or the poor-box money,

some say she had nothing with her,
neither purse nor script,

no gold-piece or silver
stamped with image of Caesar.

In any case, she struck an uncanny bargain
(or so some say) with an Arab,

a stranger in the market-place;
actually, he had a little booth of a house

set to the left, back of the market
as you pass through the lower-gate;

what he had, was not for sale; he was on his way
to a coronation and a funeral—a double affair—

what he had, his priceless, unobtainable-elsewhere
     myrrh
was for the double ceremony, a funeral and a
     throning;

his was not ordinary myrrh and incense
and anyway, it is not for sale, he said;

he drew aside his robe in a noble manner
but the un-maidenly woman did not take the hint;

she had seen nobility herself at first hand;
nothing impressed her, it was easy to see;

she simply didn't care whether he acclaimed
or snubbed her—or worse; what are insults?

she knew how to detach herself,
another unforgivable sin,

and when stones were hurled,
she simply wasn't there;

she wasn't there and then she appeared,
not a beautiful woman really—would you say?

certainly not pretty;
what struck the Arab was that she was unpredictable

this had never happened before—a woman—
well yes—if anyone did, he knew the world—a lady

had not taken a hint, had not sidled gracefully
at a gesture of implied dismissal

and with no apparent offence really,
out of the door.

It was easy to see that he was not an ordinary
     merchant;
she saw that certainly—he was an ambassador;

there was hardly anyone you could trust
with this precious merchandise,

though the jars were sealed,
the fragrance got out somehow,

and the rumour was bruited about,
even if you yourself managed to keep out

of the ordinary haunts of the merchants;
some said, this distillation, this attar

lasted literally forever, had so lasted—
though no one could of course, actually know

what was or was-not in those alabaster boxes
of the Princesses of the Hyksos Kings,

there were unguent jars, certainly;
but who would open them?

they had charms wrought upon them,
there were sigils and painted figures on all the jars

no one dismantled the tombs,
that would be wickedness—but this he knew,

his own people for centuries and centuries,
had whispered the secret of the sacred processes of
     distillation;

it was never written, not even in symbols, for this
     they knew—
no secret was safe with a woman.

She said, I have heard of you;
he bowed ironically and ironically murmured,

I have not had the pleasure,
his eyes now fixed on the half-open door;

she understood; this was his second rebuff
but deliberately, she shut the door;

she stood with her back against it;
planted there, she flung out her arms,

a further barrier,
and her scarf slipped to the floor;

her face was very pale,
her eyes darker and larger

than many whose luminous depth
had inspired some not-inconsiderable poets;

but eyes? he had known many women—
it was her hair—un-maidenly—

It was hardly decent of her to stand there,
unveiled, in the house of a stranger.

I am Mary, she said, of a tower-town,
or once it must have been towered

for Magdala is a tower;
Magdala stands on the shore;

I am Mary, she said, of Magdala,
I am Mary, a great tower;

through my will and my power,
Mary shall be myrrh;

I am Mary—O, there are Marys a-plenty,
(though I am Mara, bitter) I shall be Mary-myrrh;

I am that myrrh-tree of the gentiles,
the heathen; there are idolaters,

even in Phrygia and Cappadocia,
who kneel before mutilated images

and burn incense to the Mother of Mutilations,
to Attis-Adonis-Tammuz and his mother who was
    myrrh;

she was a stricken woman,
having borne a son in unhallowed fashion;

she wept bitterly till some heathen god
changed her to a myrrh-tree;

I am Mary, I will weep bitterly,
bitterly . . . bitterly.

But her voice was steady and her eyes were dry,
the room was small, hardly a room,

it was an alcove or a wide cupboard
with a closed door, a shaded window;

there was hardly any light from the window
but there seemed to be light somewhere,

as of moon-light on a lost river
or a sunken stream, seen in a dream

by a parched, dying man, lost in the desert . . .
or a mirage . . . it was her hair.

He who was unquestionably
master of caravans,

stooped to the floor;
he handed her her scarf;

it was unseemly that a woman
appear disordered, dishevelled;

it was unseemly that a woman
appear at all.

I am Mary, the incense-flower of the incense-tree,
myself worshipping, weeping, shall be changed to myrrh;

I am Mary, though melted away,
I shall be a tower . . . she said, Sir,

I have need, not of bread nor of wine,
nor of anything you can offer me,

and demurely, she knotted her scarf
and turned to unfasten the door.

Some say she slipped out and got away,
some say he followed her and found her,

some say he never found her
but sent a messenger after her

with the alabaster jar;
some say he himself was a Magician,

a Chaldean, not an Arab at all,
and had seen the beginning and the end,

that he was Balthasar, Melchior,
or that other of Bethlehem;

some say he was masquerading,
was an Angel in disguise

and had really arranged this meeting
to conform to the predicted pattern

which he or Balthasar or another
had computed exactly from the stars;

some say it never happened,
some say it happens over and over;

some say he was an old lover
of Mary Magdalene and the gift of the myrrh

was in recognition of an old burnt-out
yet somehow suddenly renewed infatuation;

some say he was Abraham,
some say he was God.

Anyhow, it is exactly written,
the house was filled with the odour of the ointment;

that was a little later and this was not such a small
      house
and was maybe already fragrant with boughs and
      wreaths,

for this was a banquet, a festival;
it was all very gay and there was laughter,

but Judas Iscariot turned down his mouth,
he muttered Extravagant under his breath,

for the nard though not potent,
had that subtle, indefinable essence

that lasts longer and costs more;
Judas whispered to his neighbour

and then they all began talking about the poor;
but Mary, seated on the floor,

like a child at a party, paid no attention;
she was busy; she was deftly un-weaving

the long, carefully-braided tresses
of her extraordinary hair.

But Simon the host thought,
we must draw the line somewhere;

he had seen something like this
in a heathen picture

or a carved stone-portal entrance
to a forbidden sea-temple;

they called the creature,
depicted like this,

seated on the sea-shore
or on a rock, a Siren,

a maid-of-the-sea, a mermaid;
some said, this mermaid sang

and that a Siren-song was fatal
and wrecks followed the wake of such hair;

she was not invited,
he bent to whisper

into the ear of his Guest,
I do not know her.

There was always a crowd hanging about outside
any door his Guest happened to enter;

he did not wish to make a scene,
he would call someone quietly to eject her;

Simon though over-wrought and excited,
had kept careful count of his guests;

things had gone excellently till now,
but this was embarrassing;

she was actually kissing His feet;
He does not understand;

they call him a Master,
but Simon questioned:

*this man if he were a prophet, would have known
who and what manner of woman this is.*

Simon did not know but Balthasar
or Melchior could have told him,

or better still, Gaspar or Kaspar,
who, they say, brought the myrrh;

Simon wished to avoid a scene
but Kaspar knew the scene was unavoidable

and already written in a star
or a configuration of stars

that rarely happens, perhaps once
in a little over two thousand years.

Simon could say, yes,
she looked like a heathen

picture or carved idol
from a forbidden sea-temple;

and Simon might have heard
that this woman from the city,

was devil-ridden or had been;
but Kaspar might call

the devils *daemons*,
and might even name the seven

under his breath, for technically
Kaspar was a heathen;

he might whisper tenderly, those names
without fear of eternal damnation,

Isis, Astarte, Cyprus
and the other four;

he might re-name them,
Ge-meter, De-meter, earth-mother

or Venus
in a star.

But it is not fair to compare
Kaspar with Simon;

this Simon is not Simon Peter, of course,
this is not Simon Zelotes, the Canaanite

nor Simon of Cyrene
nor the later Simon, the sorcerer,

this Simon is Simon, the leper;
but Simon being one of the band,

we presume was healed of his plague,
healed in body, while the other,

the un-maidenly mermaid, Mary of Magdala
was healed of soul; out of her, the Master

had cast seven devils;
but Simon, though healed of body,

was not conditioned to know
that these very devils or *daemons*,

as Kaspar would have called them,
were now unalterably part of the picture;

they had entered separately or together
the fair maid, perhaps not wantonly,

but crossing the threshold
of this not un-lovely temple,

they intended perhaps to pay homage,
even as Kaspar had done,

and Melchior
and Balthasar.

And Kaspar (for of course, the merchant was Kaspar)
did not at first know her;

she was frail and slender, wearing no bracelet
or other ornament, and with her scarf

wound round her head, draping her shoulders,
she was impersonal, not a servant

sent on an errand, but, as it were,
a confidential friend, sent by some great lady;

she was discretion itself
in her dark robe and head-dress;

Kaspar did not recognise her
until her scarf slipped to the floor,

and then, not only did he recognise Mary
as the stars had told (Venus in the ascendant

or Venus in conjunction with Jupiter,
or whatever he called these wandering fires),

but when he saw the light on her hair
like moonlight on a lost river,

Kaspar
remembered.

And Kaspar heard
an echo of an echo in a shell,
    in her were forgiven
    the sins of the seven
    daemons cast out of her;

and Kaspar saw as in a mirror,
another head uncovered and two crowned,

one with a plain circlet, one with a circlet of gems
which even he could not name;

and Kaspar, master of caravans,
had known splendour such as few have known,

and seen jewels cut and un-cut that altered
like water at sun-rise and sun-set,

and blood-stones and sapphires;
we need no detailed statement of Kaspar's specific
    knowledge

nor inventory of his own possessions,
all we need to know is that Kaspar

knew more about precious stones than any other,
more even than Balthasar;

but his heart was filled with a more exalted ecstasy
than any valuer over a new tint of rose or smoke-grey

in an Indian opal or pearl; this was Kaspar
who saw as in a mirror,

one head uncrowned and then one with a plain
        head-band
and then one with a circlet of gems of an inimitable colour;

they were blue yet verging on purple,
yet very blue; if asked to describe them,

you would say they were blue stones
of a curious square cut and set so that the light

broke as if from within; the reflecting inner facets
seemed to cast incalculable angles of light,

this blue shot with violet;
how convey what he felt?

he saw as in a mirror, clearly, O very clearly,
a circlet of square-cut stones on the head of a lady,

and what he saw made his heart so glad
that it was as if he suffered,

his heart laboured so
with his ecstasy.

It was not solely because of beauty
though there was that too,

it was discovery, discovery that exalted him
for he knew the old tradition, the old, old legend,

his father had had from his grandfather
and his grandfather from his great-grandfather (and so
    on),

was true; this was never spoken about, not even
    whispered in secret;
the legend was contained in old signs and symbols,

and only the most painful application could decipher
    them,
and only the very-few could even attempt to do this,

after boy-hood and youth dedicated
to the rigorous sessions of concentration

and study of the theme and law
of time-relation and retention of memory;

but in the end, Kaspar, too, received the title Magian
(it is translated in the Script, *Wise Man*).

As he stooped for the scarf, he saw this,
and as he straightened, in that half-second,

he saw the fleck of light
like a flaw in the third jewel

to his right, in the second circlet,
a grain, a flaw, or a speck of light,

and in that point or shadow,
was the whole secret of the mystery;

literally, as his hand just did-not touch her hand,
and as she drew the scarf toward her,

the speck, fleck, grain or seed
opened like a flower.

And the flower, thus contained
in the infinitely tiny grain or seed,

opened petal by petal, a circle,
and each petal was separate

yet still held, as it were,
by some force of attraction

to its dynamic centre;
and the circle went on widening

and would go on opening
he knew, to infinity;

but before he was lost,
out-of-time completely,

he saw the islands of the Blest,
he saw the Hesperides,

he saw the circles and circles of islands
about the lost centre-island, Atlantis;

he saw what the sacrosanct legend
said still existed,

he saw the lands of the blest,
the promised lands, lost;

he, in that half-second, saw
the whole scope and plan

of our and his civilization on this,
his and our earth, before Adam.

And he saw it all as if enlarged under a sun-glass;
he saw it all in minute detail,

the cliffs, the wharves, the citadel,
he saw the ships and the sea-roads crossing

and all the rivers and bridges and dwelling-houses
and the terraces and the built-up inner gardens;

he saw the many pillars and the Hearth-stone
and the very fire on the Great-hearth,

and through it, there was a sound as of many waters,
rivers flowing and fountains and sea-waves washing the
    sea-rocks,

and though it was all on a very grand scale,
yet it was small and intimate,

Paradise
before Eve . . .

And he heard, as it were, the echo
of an echo in a shell,

words neither sung nor chanted
but stressed rhythmically;

the echoed syllables of this spell
conformed to the sound

of no word he had ever heard spoken,
and Kaspar was a great wanderer,

a renowned traveller;
but he understood the words

though the sound was other
than our ears are attuned to,

the tone was different
yet he understood it;

it translated itself
as it transmuted its message

through spiral upon spiral of the shell
of memory that yet connects us

with the drowned cities of pre-history;
Kaspar understood and his brain translated:

Lilith born before Eve
and one born before Lilith,
and Eve; we three are forgiven,
we are three of the seven
daemons cast out of her.

[34]

Then as he dropped his arm
in the second half-second,

his mind prompted him,
even as if his mind

must sharply differentiate,
clearly define the boundaries of beauty;

hedges and fences and fortresses
must defend the innermost secret,

even the hedges and fortresses of the mind;
so his mind thought,

though his spirit was elsewhere
and his body functioned, though himself,

he-himself was not there;
and his mind framed the thought,

the last inner defence
of a citadel, now lost,

> *it is unseemly that a woman*
> *appear disordered, dishevelled,*

> *it is unseemly that a woman*
> *appear at all.*

What he thought was the direct contradiction
of what he apprehended;

what he saw was a woman of discretion,
knotting a scarf,

and an unpredictable woman
sliding out of a door;

we do not know whether or not
he himself followed her

with the alabaster jar; all we know is,
the myrrh or the *spikenard, very costly*, was Kaspar's,

all we know is that it was all so very soon over,
the feasting, the laughter.

And the snow fell on Hermon,
the place of the Transfiguration,

and the snow fell on Hebron
where, last spring, the anemones grew,

whose scarlet and rose and red and blue,
He compared to a King's robes,

but *even Solomon*, He said,
was not arrayed like one of these;

and the snow fell on the almond-trees
and the mulberries were domed over

like a forester's hut or a shepherd's hut
on the slopes of Lebanon,

and the snow fell
silently . . . silently . . .

And as the snow fell on Hebron,
the desert blossomed as it had always done;

over-night, a million-million tiny plants
broke from the sand,

and a million-million little grass-stalks
each put out a tiny flower,

they were so small, you could hardly
visualize them separately,

so it came to be said,
snow falls on the desert;

it had happened before,
it would happen again.

And Kaspar grieved as always,
when a single twin of one of his many goats was
     lost—

such a tiny kid, not worth thinking about,
he was such a rich man, with numberless herds,
     cattle and sheep—

and he let the long-haired mountain-goats
return to the pasture earlier than usual,

for they chafed in their pens, sniffing the air
and the flowering-grass; and he himself watched all
     night

by his youngest white camel whose bearing was
     difficult,
and cherished the foal—it looked like a large white
     owl—

under his cloak and brought it to his tent
for shelter and warmth; that is how the legend got
     about

that Kaspar
was Abraham.

He was a very kind man
and he had numberless children,

but he was not Abraham come again;
he was the Magian Kaspar;

he said *I am Kaspar,*
for he had to hold on to something;

I am Kaspar, he said when a slender girl
holding a jar, asked deferentially

if she might lower it into his well;
I am Kaspar; if her head were veiled

and veiled it almost always would be,
he would remember, though never

for a moment did he quite forget
the turn of a wrist as it fastened a scarf,

the saffron-shape of the sandal,
the pleat of the robe, the fold of the garment

as Mary lifted the latch and the door half-parted,
and the door shut, and there was the flat door

at which he stared and stared,
as if the line of wood, the rough edge

or the polished surface or plain,
were each significant, as if each scratch and mark

were hieroglyph, a parchment of incredible worth
or a mariner's map.

[40]

And no one will ever know
whether the picture he saw clearly

as in a mirror was pre-determined
by his discipline and study

of old lore and by his innate capacity
for transcribing and translating

the difficult secret symbols,
no one will ever know how it happened

that in a second or a second and half a second,
he saw further, saw deeper, apprehended more

than anyone before or after him;
no one will ever know

whether it was a sort of spiritual optical-illusion,
or whether he looked down the deep deep-well

of the so-far unknown
depth of pre-history;

no one would ever know
if it could be proved mathematically

by demonstrated lines,
as an angle of light

reflected from a strand of a woman's hair,
reflected again or refracted

a certain other angle—
or perhaps it was a matter of vibration

that matched or caught an allied
or exactly opposite vibration

and created a sort of vacuum,
or rather a *point* in time—

he called it a fleck or flaw in a gem
of the crown that he saw

(or thought he saw) as in a mirror;
no one would know exactly

how it happened,
least of all Kaspar.

No one will know exactly how it came about,
but we are permitted to wonder

if it had possibly something to do
with the vow he had made—

well, it wasn't exactly a vow,
an idea, a wish, a whim, a premonition perhaps,

that premonition we all know,
this has happened before somewhere else,

or *this will happen again—where? when?*
for, as he placed his jar on the stable-floor,

he remembered old Azar . . . old Azar
had often told how, in the time of the sudden
        winter-rain,

after the memorable autumn-drought,
the trees were mortally torn,

when the sudden frost came;
but Azar died while Kaspar was still a lad,

and whether Azar's tale referred
to the year of the yield of myrrh,

distilled in this very jar,
or another—Kaspar could not remember;

167

but Kaspar thought, there were always two jars,
the two were always together,

why didn't I bring both?
or should I have chosen the other?

for Kaspar remembered old, old Azar muttering,
other days and better ways, and it was always
      maintained

that one jar was better than the other,
but he grumbled and shook his head,

no one can tell which is which,
now your great-grandfather is dead.

It was only a thought,
someday I will bring the other,

as he placed his jar
on the floor of the ox-stall;

Balthasar had offered the spikenard,
Melchior, the rings of gold;

they were both somewhat older than Kaspar
so he stood a little apart,

as if his gift were an after-thought,
not to be compared with theirs;

when Balthasar had pushed open the stable-door
or gate, a shepherd was standing there,

well—a sort of shepherd, an older man with a staff,
perhaps a sort of night-watchman;

as Balthasar hesitated, he said, Sir,
I am afraid there is no room at the Inn,

as if to save them the trouble of coming further,
inquiring perhaps as to bedding-down

their valuable beasts; but Balthasar
acknowledged the gentle courtesy of the man

and passed on; and Balthasar entered the ox-stall,
and Balthasar touched his forehead and his breast,

as he did at the High Priest's side
before the Holy-Presence-Manifest;

and Balthasar spoke the Great Word,
and Balthasar bowed, as if the weight of this honour

bent him down, as if over-come
by this overwhelming Grace,

and Balthasar stood aside
and Melchior took his place.

———————————

And Melchior made gesture with his hands
as if in a dance or play,

to show without speaking, his unworthiness,
to indicate that this, his gift, was symbolic,

worthless in itself (those weighty rings of gold),
and Melchior bent and kissed the earth, speechless,

for this was the ritual
of the second order of the priests.

———————————

And Kaspar stood a little to one side
like an unimportant altar-servant,

and placed his gift
a little apart from the rest,

to show by inference
its unimportance in comparison;

and Kaspar stood
he inclined his head only slightly,

as if to show,
out of respect to the others,

these older, exceedingly honoured ones,
that his part in this ritual

was almost negligible,
for the others had bowed low.

But she spoke so he looked at her,
she was shy and simple and young;

she said, Sir, it is a most beautiful fragrance,
as of all flowering things together;

but Kaspar knew the seal of the jar was unbroken.
he did not know whether she knew

the fragrance came from the bundle of myrrh
she held in her arms.

London
December 18-31, 1944.